Wine-Dark Mother
and the
Trapper's Son

Wine-Dark Mother and the Trapper's Son

illustrated second edition

Jim Churchill-Dicks

Printed in the United States of America.

For more information, or to book an event, contact :

j.churchill.dicks@gmail.com

http://musehickpublications.com

First Edition cover image by Jason Andrew Wilson

Used with permission

ISBN — 978-1-953527-59-2

First Edition: 2016

Illustrated Second Edition, 2024

For Carol, who entered into the cave and held my hand, and also for my mothers and my fathers.

Praise for *Wine-Dark Mother and the Trapper's Son*

"Beast angel/I present this psalm by hand." Writes Jim Churchill-Dicks in his moving debut. Angels are terrifying, Rilke tells us, but Churchill-Dicks sees both the angelic and the terror in ourselves, our families, our passions. There is a real pain and real poise in these lines of a man who admits: "I see the bruise roping/Cordelia's throat, as she rises/for her applause."

The knowledge that comes with such seeing is anguished: "I have witnessed God's absence," he tells us (as we also whisper to ourselves) and yet with all anguish there comes tenderness: "I have witnessed God's presence. Musk behind a lover's ear." So what does this poet teach us? Anguish, yes, but also of the joy in the sensual moment, in the beloved's body, and so even when the speaker sees a scar, he admits "I love to trace this scar/with the tip of my nose." He also shares with us his sense of a nourishing, dizzying natural world: "I watch my mother planting/alyssum, indigo/lobelia, the bulbs/of lavender tulips, he/clipped nails christened/in earth."

In the end, Jim Churchill-Dicks makes me think of the great Brazilian poet Carlos Drummond de Andrade who wrote of "a portrait of a family travelling through flesh." The word "travelling" is crucial here, as Churchill-Dicks truly undergoes a journey in this book's arc. From anger to forgiveness travel the images of his poems, and when the book ends in two final, glorious poems, "Revocation" and "Farewell Poem to a Living Father," I am deeply moved.

-Ilya Kaminsky
National Book Award Nominee, *Deaf Republic*

"Behold, the unmaking of a chosen son." In Jim Churchill-Dicks' *Wine-Dark Mother and the Trapper's Son*, the poet unmakes himself- shedding grief and the recriminations of a difficult father- to evoke a deep and lasting grace.

These poems are vivid and muscular and lit as if by lightning. In the extraordinary "Jacob Wrestling," Churchill-Dicks breaks in and out of prose, the intercessions as urgent and profound as their address: "You stain me into silence./Bleach my bones, beloved./Let me be your breath again."

Tender, furious, vulnerable, and sometimes hilarious, the book arcs toward a hard-won forgiveness: the unmaking of the chosen son, the birth of a good man.

-Katie Farris
Standing in the Forest of Being Alive

Jim Churchill-Dicks' poetry collection *Wine-Dark Mother and the Trapper's Son* witnesses the explosive landscapes of fractured families with a level gaze as tender as it is reckoning.

The ill-loved child craves reconciliation the adults around them are not equipped to provide; these poems excavate the journey into adulthood that requires each of us to reconcile with ourselves and our fractured histories, when it is already too late. Here is truth-telling and compassion for our father's and mother's failures- and our own. The mother, observed asleep: "Is she dead?" ... "Do not wake up./This is who you/want to be. This is who your promised you'd be." The father, "peeling his orange flight-suit halfway down, a snake shedding skin...'I lost him,' ... 'My boy has augured in' ... intermittent street lights staining his warm, wet face."

Tectonic violence jerks the ground under these poems. Recurring images of smoke, ash, volcanic eruptions, and what we see in the plumes create an ominous and contested beauty: "Spirit, what do you want?/What do you want me to know/among these yellow leaves?" Contrasts with hollow despair: "That plume is a woman/who just couldn't take any more."

As the collection progresses, the images begin to cohere into a larger sky-scape of un-easy forgiveness. There are no shortcuts here, no platitudes, in place of real integration: "Whatever we say no to/comes back and sticks/to us a little bit" ... "And herein lies the revocation, /the cancellation of the debt." In the final piece of the collection, "Farewell Poem to a Living Father," Churchill-Dicks closes the journey precisely where and how it must be closed: "take this folded paper/and give it to the boatman/when he asks you/if you were loved."

Few writers have either the courage or the capacity for specificity that is required to tell the complex truth of a family's immense cruelties, or its fragile loves. In *Wine-Dark Mother and the Trapper's Son*, Churchill-Dicks reminds us of the fact, that in Jewish tradition, witness is an active verb; a difficult praxis, and a real action toward reconstituting the world, and making whole what was scattered. In these poems' reconstitution of memory, soul and family, we are enabled to more fiercely and truly witness our own.

-Jessamyn Smyth
The Inugami Mochi and *Gilgamesh Wilderness*

Contents

Every day, all of us here, we're building gods that have gone rampant, and it's time we started knocking them down and forgetting their names.

-Chris Abani

If a tree falls in the forest and no one is there to hear it, will your next poem still be about your dad?

　　　　　　　　　　　　　　　　　-Sparrow

Invocation: Post Patri
(after the opening of the Holy Quran)

1 How does an unbeliever call upon the name of God, an unbeliever's tongue-spilt profanity in even the pretty syllables, profanity compared to the angel's tongues, in comparison to the wholeness of stones? How does a desert wanderer test the generosity of the one most merciful of us all?   2 What is the worth of an infidel's thanks and praise, thanks and praise to the Maker and Shepherd of all? The one who connects us all, the one who connects all things, who connects these stones into the backbones of our fathers, 3 the one whose generosity is a stone made into bread- whose mercy is blood unmade into water. 4 To you, O worthy judge, the one with authority over the living and the dead, I fall to the hem of your robe. 5 To you, (Alone) I bathe your feet. To you (The Most Lonely) I kiss my tears upon your feet, and ask you for your help 6 to be my shepherd. Be my guide. To lead me on the path, 7 the canyon's cleavage that leads to a river of these bleached stones, not (the wayward path) of those who are seemingly cruel (such as my father) or of those (such as me) who seem to betray their fathers.

Ovation for King Lear

I see the bruise roping
Cordelia's throat, as she rises
for her applause.

To speak our hearts to our fathers,
or to show mercy upon them
and utter a pregnant
"Nothing."

Fire

Through the curtains
I watch my father leave
us. I bring you a glass
of water. You shudder
and sigh, drink it down

smiling.

You cup the back of my neck
with tapered fingers,
harmless nails. Why

mother, when I remember,
those curtains are on fire

and you collapse onto the carpet,
face buried, wailing
for the both of us, a cry

that I cannot extinguish?

Ashes

The elder gods knew that a fire as hot as the sun smouldered deep beneath the earth, sometimes burning through its crust and into the bowels of mountains—

Bernard Evslin, "The Sirens"

I. 1953

My mother, three years old, gallops in the garden
behind her grandmother. Mt. St. Helens,
a smiling Buddha, is plopped above the morning
sheet of clouds, a frosty dome.

"Ice cream!" my mother squeals,
while plucking green tomatoes
without rebuke, only a sigh
from her grandmother,

Bless your little heart, Suzie.

Fanny's harsh words
are only meant for Pappy,
her husband, and for the occasional slugs
who slime their promiscuous way
through her nasturtiums, alyssum and smiling pansies—

Fanny takes pleasure
cursing these creatures, my mother
close behind, pouring Pappy's Olympia
beer over their shriveling bodies,
and then [for good measure] sheering them
in half with rusty garden scissors.

II. 1958

At the kitchen table, a carton of Newports
beside the cookie jar, Fanny chain-smokes
and tells stories. Suzie munches on cookies.

Fanny's stories are always the same,
about her sons fighting at sea in World War II,
Suzie's two uncles who saw active combat
while her father, the youngest, played football
for the Army in Nevada, fighting what he called
"The Battle of Las Vegas."

Fanny always laughs at this part. *Can you believe
that Suzie? The God-bless-it battle of Las Vegas!*

Recovering, Fanny flicks the long ash
from her cigarette, takes a drag, while
my mother concentrates on the thin
trail of smoke, curling upward
from the glowing coal. She makes out shapes
like watching clouds in the sky.

There's a mouse, a knight, a woman tied to the tracks.

III. 1973

Suzie lives in a thin yellow trailer now,
a Marine Corps wife fighting
The Battle of Pensacola. *Bless her heart.*
She rocks me to sleep, brushing my wet hair
from a fever, breaking. My father stops briefly
in the lit doorway, casting his silhouette before
heading out again for the night.

At least you are good at being a mother, he says,
and as he thuds down the hall toward the front door.

Suzie remembers overhearing his mother at their wedding,
Oh, I'm sure she got pregnant on purpose, and
That dirty woman has taken my only son away from me—

As we hear my father's truck spray gravel
from the driveway, my mother rocks me,
her only son, and whispers *You son of a bitch*,

I will be the best mother in the whole wide world.

IV. 1978

Suzie answers on the third ring; her eight-year-old son
visiting her ex-husband's house, a six-hour drive north.
She hears conspiratorial whispering in the background
and then her son, *I want to live with my dad from now on.*

Absolutely not, her voice level and cool, then hangs up
the phone, grabs her keys and hucks them against the wall.
The keychain stabs into the drywall and hangs there.

She winces, cradles her abdomen, a fleshy dome,
eight months pregnant. The low heels of her shoes
click with purpose toward the new hole she has made.

He's become just like his father. She yanks out her keys,
shakes them and storms out through the door.
She revs the engine of her Datsun too high, and squeals
out of the driveway, heading north.

V. May 18, 1980

What's left of my family stands
on the higher ground of Fanny's garden
where at six years old I witnessed
Fanny's war with slugs myself.

Same flashing eyes. Same scissors. But salt
instead of beer, since Pappy was in heaven.

These days, Fanny's garden is neglected,
her lungs filling with fluid. She is drowning
from the stories of too many ashes.

The family watches the long spectacle
of Mt. St. Helens erupting. My brother
and I look for shapes in the megaton plume.

My brother shouts, *Broccoli!* I proclaim, *A brain!*
Fanny gives a gravelly hoot, *'At's usin' your noodle, boys!*

My mother gazes red-eyed at the mountain.
No boys, she whispers,

That plume is a woman who just couldn't take anymore—

25

Snoopyland

It wasn't all *that* bad.
Not everyone got to go
to a kindergarten
named *Snoopyland*.

1. I am the Fonz

It is the year my mother finds a new husband. They honeymoon in Monte-
rey. All I get is a t-shirt- lettered in glitter blue marquee which reads, "The
Fonz". I am five, and still know how to make the best of things, so with my
hair slicked back, and mirrored sun glasses at the table, I exclaim "Sit on it!"
when the new man of the house tells me to finish my mashed potatoes.

The Fonz does NOT! Dig. Spankings--

"Heeeeeyyyyyyy," I howl on the playground and strut around Snoopyland,
"Whoaa!" I growl to Bonnie, my classmate chum and teacher's daughter,
as she grabs my hand and pulls me under the rusted twirly slide. I hold my
breath as she kisses me, our lips clamped shut as she hums,
"hmmmmmmmmmmmm" for as long as she can breathe, then seperates- a
sloppy, dramatic, "muahhh!" Giggles and more giggles as she runs away.

Twitterpated, love inflated- the Fonz. Digs. Chicks.

Bonnie's shoulder touches mine as we melt crayons on a hot plate, and as
we churn cream into cottage cheese, I lose my cool,   my eyes
dopey. The Fonz is dead. He's jumped the shark and
my heart wants to bust with music. I trade in the
Fonz for a sea-blue suit. A leisure suit, but don't be
fooled. Things are about to get serious.

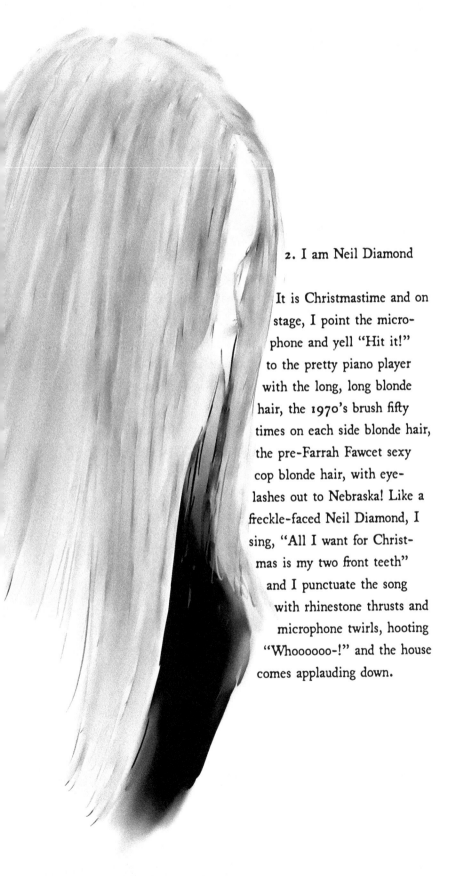

2. I am Neil Diamond

It is Christmastime and on
stage, I point the micro-
phone and yell "Hit it!"
to the pretty piano player
with the long, long blonde
hair, the 1970's brush fifty
times on each side blonde hair,
the pre-Farrah Fawcet sexy
cop blonde hair, with eye-
lashes out to Nebraska! Like a
freckle-faced Neil Diamond, I
sing, "All I want for Christ-
mas is my two front teeth"
and I punctuate the song
with rhinestone thrusts and
microphone twirls, hooting
"Whoooooo-!" and the house
comes applauding down.

3. I am Charlie Brown

Spring comes too soon and Bonnie now loves
David. As I Charlie Brown my way to my
mother's car after school her AM radio croons
Mathis. Before we leave the lot, I am bawling
in snotty stutters, my mother asks,

"What's the matter with you?"

I point to the radio, and shout "Mo-om!" as if
she were a four-letter word.

"Feelings!"

4. I Write the Songs

I ain't been alive forever, but I know my first
favorite song. The pretty piano player knows it
too, because I sing it alone on the playground.
During nap time she places the tune on my
chest. I'm wearing a Hulk t-shirt, though I try
real hard not to smash things.

I write the songs that make the whole world sing.

"That will be you someday", she whispers. She musses
my hair. "You'll make all the young girls cry."

I don't remember her name, but let's call her
April, since that is the month I leave. My father
is waiting for me in Florida. On the last day,
April gives me her hippy guitar,
with the macramé strap, the hand-painted
fretboard of peace signs and smiles.

"Write those songs Jimmy Dicks."

She snuffles and hugs me. I nod, my face
in her hair, but I don't wanna make anyone
cry.

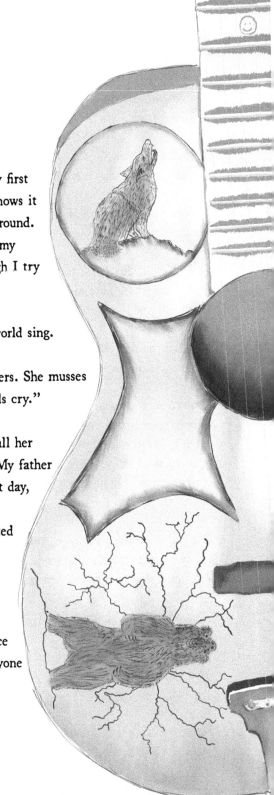

Jacob Wrestling
from the bronze series by Tim Holmes

I.

I have witnessed God's absence. A satchel bloated with letters
addressed RETURN TO SENDER.

I have witnessed God's presence. Musk behind a lover's ear,
a slow-moving tear tapping her silken pillow. Yet

a seasoned pilgrim knows that beneath an angel's song
can churn the crazed appetite of a beast who devours her young.

Why should this lamentation be of any interest? A fleshy pink boy
conquering pink boy, marching pink boy? I have witnessed through
both sides of the curtain, witnessed a household crumbling down.

Behold, the unmaking of a chosen son.
To you, ghost angel, beast angel, I present this psalm by hand.

Do not send your prophets anymore.
I have closed their mouths, consumed them all
page by page, bone by bone you
green-leaved shapeshifter,
voyeur, corn husk of a lover—
Meet me here in the mud.

Your hounds circle my legs, wet nosed jabbing between my legs.
They know me, know my scent. They howl a name, a language
like my hidden tongue. I am waiting. Waiting. Show yourself.

The hounds are panting
patient patient patient
Splash of footpads from behind me,
your glowing figure strikes.

2.

Your palm claps the back of my neck
my neck with elbows twisting
shoulders roll and writhe
into a massive thud
of steam. A slap,
a shock—

slow sinking, deep into a thickened pool
where limbs untangle, no more breath—

Near suffocation: music. A kaleidoscope
of color, from clay to ashes, from embers
glowing to flames becoming the tree
again. To sprouting leaf and blossom.
Ripened fruit.

I see your broad lips begin to part
to cover mine, *to bless me?*

The stepmother is eating her young while my father rushes to his woman,
to all of his women because his mother my grandmother has chosen me
over him over his children over his new woman who eats her young.

No one told me she was dying.

Grandmother was dying, a hospice bed
in her living room, a morphine drip,
for weeks an increasing dosage. No one
told me father's woman wiped his mother's brow,
eyes flashing with performative glee.

My father called when she was dead.
Told me she was dead, didn't say her ashes
were already scattered, a wreath already
dropped into the sea, by helicopter
into the sea, though I *love* my grandmother's son,

and even more, I love his son, my half brother.
There is no race, no birthright to earn, or to take.
It is freely forfeit. But our mothers keep eating their young.

O angel, your lips are parted,
wet and hungry, *to bless me?*

I'm not done with you.

Entwined again,
we rise above the greasy crust.

3.

Gasping air again, cacophonies
of slapping bodies. Anxious hounds,
noses vaulted heavenward,
howl with their entire bodies:

I am the chosen son,
the chosen witness to my
mother's inconsolable wailing.
Her flight, curled into a knot,
behind her bedroom door.

Her fight, nails drawn,
a lack of recognition
over friend or foe.

I become the chosen enemy,
red crescents weeping
down my impotent forearms,
my hapless neck. I am the chosen
pink chosen pig-pup screeching at the moon—

And then, dear God, I've gained an upper hand
upon your jaw, O angel, and I push you back
into the clay where I still belong.
No interrogation. No *why did you allow this?*
No *how could you allow this?*
Just my knee into your spine,
your face pressed in the clay,
your breath almost gone.

I could finish this
don't let me finish this
my flesh, your flesh.

Behold, a flash of light beginning from my hip—

5.

Consciousness. You are gone.
Your hounds are gone,
but our tracks are everywhere.

I cover my eyes.
I place my hand over my mouth.

I have stalked the corridors of language
and today I find them empty.

I have been infused by you.
By this absence, this presence,
this light of morning.

You stain me into silence.
Bleach my bones beloved.

Let me be your breath again.

How Grandmother Said Goodbye

A family cloaked in secrets
must learn subtext to survive:
the earnest hug, her added rouge,
but most of all

the way she stood, gazed
through curtains to the curb,
smiled and whispered
for some stranger's pickup truck

to come and haul her away.

Our Father

He extended his routine flight
and flew above our camp, hovered
there in his rumbling chariot as we ran
to the lake shore to greet him, waved
and hollered to this pillared cloud of God and angels.

He circled behind the trees,
a thundering perimeter, a whirring proclamation,

I am that I am and you are mine!

But my father
was just another father
in an airship fleet of fathers

                        perpetually whirring away—

Icarus

Little brothers—
Fearless, wish to fill
their fathers' empty flight jackets.

Not yet worshipped
they dream of hovering
above the world
much like hummingbirds

though grandiose in size,
thundering like helos,
small faces thrust heavenward
rising horribly toward the sun.

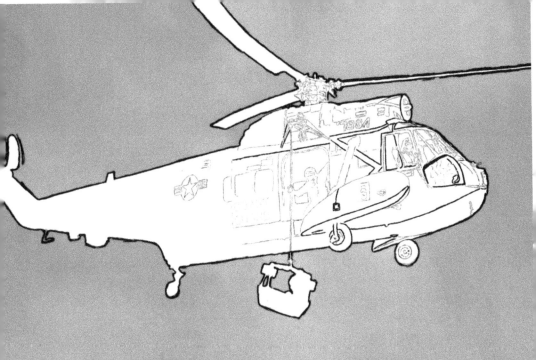

A Crack of Light

I remember my father at dawn,
dragging his heavy boots across
the threshold, peeling his or-
ange flight suit halfway down,
a snake shedding his skin as he
chugged milk from the light of
the open refrigerator. I watched
him from behind the swinging
kitchen door as he told his wife
about his recent case. *We lost
him*, he says.

*Twenty foot seas, winds at 50 knots,
only five-foot of rotor clearance on
either side. Was the water's temp
that killed him, though.*

His voice was tired, without emo-
tion. Not like when, on that same
summer visit, I watched him from
the back seat as he sobbed behind
the wheel like an engine chok-
ing in and out of gear while we
listened to how Thurman Munson,
his favorite Yankees catcher had
perished in an airplane crash.

Augered in, he cried. *My boy has
augered in*, and I watched him
through the rearview mirror, the
intermittent streetlights staining
his warm, wet face.

Son of Abraham

A boy and a man walk into a bar and yes, the boy is me. I am zits and freckles. An Adam's Apple with a Dorothy Hamill haircut. It is 1983 and I am wearing my favorite Deff Leppard Union Jack shirt with cutoff sleeves to showcase my noodle arms.

The man is my father or was my father depending on what your definition of *is* is. He grabs my bicep hard and says, *Wow, you're pretty strong... pretty ugly and strong smelling,* then holds his nose and laughs at himself laughing at me. *It's just a joke,* he says, *don't be so sensitive,* he says. Well, I've got a joke for you.

A father and son walk into a bar which doubles as a café/country store. A bear of a man squats at a table slurping stew, and the woman he's with is cold-eyed and smoking Salems, but the boy first notices her high cutoff jean shorts and that she's not wearing any underpants and for propriety's sake let's just say that there is something going on down there that resembles Reagan's Vice President. And speaking of that, the bear man has a homunculus beard that nearly reaches the table and that also impresses the boy since his Grandpa Dick recently told him that at this point, the boy has less peach fuzz than his grandmother.

We're all a bunch of comedians.

Now Cecilville, California is the heart of Mary Jane country back then, which at the time is still illegal, and being a sheltered suburbanite, the boy is clueless. And that's where they are, in the heart of the Trinity Alps. The father is wearing a ball cap which is likely a bit disconcerting to the café patrons. He's been a big fan of Bill Murray since the movie *Stripes*, so he also enjoys *Ghostbusters* by association. The cap has an embroidered marijuana leaf with a red circle and a slash. "Budbusters" it reads, from one of his drug interdiction missions in the Coast Guard. Cymbal splash. No one in the tavern-café-country store is laughing.

The man grabs the boy's shoulder and faces him toward the bar. A prospector calling himself Jasper sidles up to the two of them. He is a red tattered flannel shirt, a missing tooth. He is moldy tobacco. The boy and the man are Johnny Cash and baseball diamonds. Jasper notices the man's ball cap, scowls, points at the hat and asks *what's your business?* My father looks hard at the prospector, looks hard at the boy looking at himself in a Budweiser mirror, answers, *we're heading for the upper meadows of Grizzly Lake.*

You best stay on the trail, Jasper says. The tavern-café-country store grows eerily still. The man can feel the hairy local eyeballing the boy.

*

Father and son arrive at the trailhead, an unmarked steep chute wedged between a tall stand of thick evergreens. The boy's towering black Jansport back bulges at the zippers. Straps grind heavy and unfamiliar against his shoulders. The steep grade of the trail tests his buckling thighs, his young feet stuffed into new waffle-stompers squeaking under this newfound weight.

In the distance, the boy listens for his father's feet and focuses on these sounds, to imitate their rhythm, attempting to inherit their strength. Once his body has taken on this cadence, his mind retreats- while he pushes higher with each arduous step- retreats into thoughts of baseball, and his red shirted teammates sponsored by the Rock Creek Tavern.

These are the guys who laugh with me any time I am third in the batting order with our head coach bellowing *Ellias is up! Macki on deck! Dicks in the hole!* Snickers and guffaws, especially from the big bikers in the stands who are our sponsors.

And oh my God how those leather-crested yard birds go berserk when I hit that accidental Grand Slam, my helmet slipping over my eyes in mid swing, the singing aluminum tink lifting my helmet to see the ball magically soar over the fence as I round the bases, one hand pressed down against my helmet, my other arm churning wildly, unable to stifle my excited giggles and turning toward home awash in sweaty, red polyester shirts and high fives and cheering boys who smell like clover and copper pennies and they were chanting *Jimmy Dicks, Jimmy Dicks Jimmy Dicks* and before I realize it I'm letting my stepfather, Hutch, hug me at home plate.

The boy hears rushing water. His father turns to him and says, *we're just about to the lower meadows... you're doing well.* The boy realizes that this is the longest stretch that they have ever not talked to one another while sharing the same space. He goes for a year at a time without hearing from his dad in an absence long enough to think that the man has forgotten about him entirely, so each rare time they are together, the boy can't keep his mouth shut. Now though, the boy seems better able to occupy the silence in his own head.

The rocky knolls to the lower meadows hold thousands of wildflowers, most prominently the crimson Indian Paintbrush and the lavender blossomed spheres of wild onions in bloom, and countless nameless others grip tenaciously to the bulbous creek-side rocks. While taking closeup pictures from his borrowed camera, the boy hears a nearby stomping in the bushes. He looks up just in time to see the tail end of a baby black bear, rapidly scampering away. The man notices also and scowls. *We'd better be moving on* he says as he scans the nearby tree line, then smiles in a way that seems strange to the boy. *You can guarantee that bear's mama is somewhere near watching us.*

Meandering along the rising creek, they finally make it to
the upper meadows in twilight. Both hungry, the man kills
a toad with the found rusty metal file, hucking the file like
a throwing knife and impales the toad in mid-jump. Cheers.
The man carves the toad's legs into slimy bite sized chunks
and gives them to his son who tosses them into a small
kettle with boiling water, bullion and wild onions found in
the meadow. While waiting for dinner, the boy rummages
through the man's survival kit and sees a small
vacuum-packed wrapper. He tries to pronounce a familiar
yet unfamiliar word. *What's a cone dome?* the man looks at
his son holding a condom in his hand *it's pronounced con-
dom.* The boy stares blankly back, *what does it do?* The man
stifles a laugh, looks awkwardly at his son then looks away.
*What's the matter with you? Haven't you ever heard of a
rubber before?*

In the shock of adrenaline, the boy stabs the rubber back
into the survival kit and is all *yeah of course I mean totally
I mean yeah, I know what a rubber is...* The boy stammers
like an idiot, mortified as if he has failed some manly rite of
passage even though he's been studying this nonsense for like
Dude, he has been joking about rubbers with his buddies for
the past year and a half. You know, like the one about Dairy
Queen getting pregnant because Burger King forgot to wrap
his whopper? He and his buddies are rubber aficionados, they
have just- never seen one before. In his head, the boy imag-
ines a rubber looking more like one of those big ole novelty
latex finger puppets with googly eyes and gangly arms and
with a brilliant blue or green latex fur, covered with Mup-
pet-like rubber spines. *Fun, right?* Confronted with its true
form, the boy is disappointed. He can't understand what all
the fuss is about. In his father's package, it looks more like
an already chewed piece of bubble gum. *Lame!*

Later as father and son are nestled in their sleeping bags, a herd of eight deer wanders close enough to touch them. One doe starts licking a nearby patch of ground where the boy had urinated. The boy looks silently at his father; nose crinkled in disgust. *They do that for the salt.* Soon after the man speaks, a lone buck arrives on the nearby snowbank and flurries his antlers. The does scatter in the twilight.

Flat on their backs in their sleeping bags, looking skyward, the boy and the man are surrounded by a stand of old growth Douglas firs, rising like pillars toward the emerging stars. *Now that's a cathedral* the man says.

*

Morning. Father and son wake up to frost on their sleeping bags. They dress quickly, ready to tackle the unmarked scramble to the shore of Grizzly Lake. Leaving their packs behind, the man's scans the slope looking for the most likely route. He points to a rock chute well north of the lake. *It'll take longer* he says *and we'll have to cross that high snowfield but it looks less steep than if we follow that nose of rock by the waterfall.*

As the man begins to navigate through the narrow tree branches and granite boulders of the cliff washout, the chute grows much less stable and steeper by the step. The boy scrambles to stay on pace with his father who seems driven to find his goal. Three hundred feet above the meadow, a boulder gives way from under the boy's feet creating an avalanche of rock, tumbling, leaping, and crashing toward the valley floor. The boy barely manages to grip a larger boulder ahead of him, with his fingertips pawing at the unyielding surface as he begins to lose purchase.

Dad!

Time seems to slow as the boy watches the back of his father's flannel shirt ahead of him. The slow turn of the man's head, the beginning of a hand reached out but hopelessly beyond the boy's reach, the man's eyes filling with a slow dread *or was it curiosity?*

The boy's body grips to a halt just before losing it and somersaulting backwards down the chute to his certain death. His fingertips are peeled and stinging, and blood slowly rises to the surface. The man steps his full weight down onto a boulder which thankfully holds, grasps the boy by the back of his flannel shirt and lifts him to his feet. *That was close* the man says, smiling.

I want to come down, the boy says in a higher-pitched voice than he wishes, but he's scared enough to show it and not back down.

Nah, the man says, brushing off the boy.

It's more dangerous going down than it is going up. He looks to the skyline and points upward. *If we continue all the way up this chute to the ridge and then cut across that snowfield to the lake, we could probably find a safer return route from the waterfall.* The boy feels he has no choice but to follow and watches the man's confident climbing footsteps, some of which dislodge a shower of small then medium stones in his wake, pelting the boy's shins then tumble down to upturn larger stones vaulting down again in jarring distant crashes that set the boy's heart thrumming like a flock of sparrows.

And speaking of birds, here's a bird joke. This one time at the mall, my stepdad Hutch convinces me in the rushing thoroughfare or whatever you call it in front of the pet store that a cockatoo, like the cool one in Baretta is talking TO ME. I am eight and my stepdad is right behind me, imitating the big white bird, *Hey Jim,* he says. *Do your homework, be good to your brother and quit picking your nose.* I am in awe, like *how do you know my name!?* Passersby are laughing and I don't catch on until years later when Hutch divulges at a family dinner to raucous laughter from everybody, including his big old donkey laugh and even me laughing too. I'm all *that bird knew EVERYTHING about me!*

But as I was saying, the vast and steep snow face meets them at the top of the ridge, which descends like a broad white shoulder of ice and snow between themselves and the lake, still far in the distance. Parched, the boy plunges his face into the course, summer snow, crunching and melting the snow in his mouth. *Don't do that* the man says *that will just make you more dehydrated*. His son whines that he's thirsty. *Then we'll have to get to the waterfall, won't we? Get up and let's go.*

Heat bears down from the noontime cloudless sky, sapping away the boy's energy with each crunching step. They have not brought water with them because the man thought it would be a good idea to trust their ability to find the lake quickly. They have not brought food with them because the man believed it would be an adventure to believe in fish from the lake. From this higher viewpoint, the boy can see that Grizzly Lake, like Hell apparently, is still frozen over.

Step crunch step crunch the boy's imagination dries up into the present reality that one misstep could cause him to slide down again- slide down the snow slope this time and over the steep cliff at the end of the snow face. The man kicks sturdy steps into the snow for the boy to follow. He is far ahead of the boy, determined for the lake.

Step crunch step crunch minutes slip into hours. The marching sun keeps bearing down, then reflects even more potently off the snow and into their eyes. The boy's face stings pink and is burning. The hard slope tilts against them. The lake appears to keep its distance even with each stride toward it like some mirage. *Step crunch step crunch* no progress no water no food too much sun. As the boy wipes his forehead, perspiration sluices through his eyebrows and courses into his stinging eyes. He trudges through this snow, this desert toward his desert father leading him through the wilderness *toward what? toward sacrifice? toward what?* The boy remembers the words to a song his mother played over and over on the turntable,

-through your love and through the ram
you saved the son of Abraham—

The sun grows further into the western sky.

Without ceremony, without talking, the man and the boy stumble through the thick stand of dense compact fur branches, scratching into the boy's pink forearms and cheeks and finally to the lake. Although the lake is frozen with a thick skim of ice covering the surface, the base of the shore has thawed. At his feet, a dead fish, bloated on its side, floats and lists in the shallow eddy. The nearby waterfall spills outward into the yawning oblivion out of sight. Down at the water's edge, knees almost touching, father and son cup their hands and eagerly drink their fill. The icy water shocks and soothes the boy's burnt face, his leather-dry throat.

Later, at the cliff's edge, the boy, who is still compounded by the gravity of his fear, like a gyroscope pressing him down to the face of the rock, snake-crawls on his belly to the edge of the waterfall's cliff, his curiosity winning out. He peers over the side, looks down to the valley floor then back to the top of the falls. His eyes follow one drop flying at a time, vaulting outside of the water's course then arcing downward falling out of sight -*as the dungeon starts to fall,* he remembers from his Deff Leppard cassette tape,

-*and it's too late too late too late for love*—

*

As the boy and the man begin their journey down, the man tries to find a safer path by stepping down by the waterfall. The boulder washout toward the falls turns out to be even more treacherous than the northern route. *We're gonna have to go part way across the snow slope again* the man says. The boy moans but keeps it to himself and reluctantly follows. Crunching slowly across the snow, inch by inch, the sun begins to move closer toward the horizon. The man squints at his son, irritated, *We're going to have to move faster than the way you're moving. We are running out of light.*

The man spots a possible route just below the snowfield. *That might work as long as it doesn't cliff out past that stand of trees,* he says pointing at a chute between themselves and the waterfall. He begins to step down the slope. The man doesn't get ten feet down before he loses his footing and lands on his backside. *Whoa!*

The man begins to slide and pick up speed. He doesn't even seem to be attempting to stop. He makes no sound as he rapidly slides down the face toward the massive cliff. The boy is amazed and horrified and angry that his father is not even trying to stop himself. *Dad!*

The man is growing closer to the edge now, 200 yards downhill from his son, rifling down the slope, spitting a wake of course snow behind him. Without a scream, silent and calm, the man is there, and then the man is gone.

The boy stands frozen. There is no sound but the nearby waterfall, a light breeze worrying his ears. There is no music in the boy's head. There is barely breath in his lungs. The boy's eyes are locked on the exact place where his father had disappeared.

The man is gone.

Alone, as the sun dips below the western Ridge, the boy has no other choice in his mind but to follow. *I'm coming Dad*, the boy says, resigned. He begins to take a step downward. The slick summer snow is beginning to give way. *I'm right behind you.* The boy scans down the snow face to the vast and broken emptiness awaiting him, compressing the valley below.

It's at that moment that I begin to feel this terrible invisible presence, pressing in, interested yet indifferent to my impending mortality, much like that time at recess in 6th grade. All the girls skip outside while me and the boys watch Joey Martini feed his pet boa constrictor. We circle and cheer, me and the boys, waiting for the kill- the haunted look on the mouse's face, it's frantic pawing against the glass and rock, the boa's omnipotent unfeeling stare. And how eventually the mouse halts, shuddering in the glass corner. Finally in a strike of boiling coils the victim's tiny jaws squeeze open. Its eyes fade from pink to black while we watch, stunned silent, unable to look away. We lose time as the boa takes its time to swallow its prey. And when only the mouse's tail and furry hind legs are left, our teacher appears. He presides over us trembling boys and joins in the waning spectacle, and speaks hoarsely of Mother Nature and of getting used to it—

Getting used to it the boy whispers, two small feet wedged precariously on holy ground, beginning to give way—

Then far down the slope, movement, small yet certain at the cliff's edge. The black dot of what could be a head, and then definitely, the man's flannel arm waving, followed by a faint shout, *Hey I think I found the trail! It sure as hell ain't thisaway!*

You sonofabitch, the boy blurts out with sudden jarring sobs as he runs disjointedly toward his father in unheeding, skidding steps. The crunching snow muffles the sound of his cries. *I hate you. I hate you I hate you—*

As he skids closer, the boy can see the man trapped in an eight-foot-deep snow moat melted out by the presence of a lone squatty fur just yards away from the cliff's actual edge. The man's leg was rammed into one of its narrowed limbs with such force that it had briefly knocked him unconscious. His thigh is now badly swollen, straining against his blue jeans.

The boy wishes, he *wishes* that either God or this invisible presence which was about to eat him whole would have appeared to the man in all their divine glory and bellowed to his face-

Behold, this is Jimmy Dicks you careless fop! And you are not the only one he belongs to!

The sun is well below the western sheer rock face, and the sky is progressively darkening. At the lip of the snow pit, the boy grasps the man's forearm, grunting and with all his strength and with the man's help, pulls him up from the moat. The boy does not even fake amusement to the man's joking smile. *I saw you disappear I-* the boy looks away barely able to breathe. The man can see that his son is trying not to cry. *Well, we're not out of the woods yet* he says.

Together, with one arm draped around the boy, the man hobbles, slides, and trips down the rest of the mountainside trying to avoid the ankle breaking roots and boulders in the failing light. The white granite takes on an unearthly lavender glow.

Growing closer to the campsite, the boy and the man can smell a stranger's fire and pungent bacon grease. It's fully night by the time they reach the campfire, and reflected by the light of the flames, they recognize Jasper, the old prospector from Cecilville.

*

How you doing boys? Jasper garbles out with a mouth full of bacon and mashed potatoes. The man straightens up, attempting to mask his injury. The boy stands directly beside him, exhausted and hungry. *Getting by* the man manages, *how long have you been here?* Jasper spits into the fire. *Long enough to see the whole goddamn spectacle.* He points out to the nearby cliff now invisible in the dark. *Thought y'all were done for, sliding down like that.* He rubs his face with greasy fingers. *Almost were, anyway. I thought you might like some real mountain food.*

They settle tentatively next to Jasper on a fallen log and accept his offer. They eat quietly and eagerly while Jasper spins grandiose lies about panning for gold, and about checking his claim at a nearby abandoned homestead called Bob's Farm.

After the fire has died down and Jasper has finally run out of verbal steam, they all settle into their sleeping bags and the men fall asleep quickly. The boy remains awake, next to the man, wary of the night. For the first time, he felt protective of the man. He had never seen him so physically vulnerable until this moment. The man had leaned on him for the rest of his hobbled way down the mountain. The boy could still feel that weight on his shoulders.

> And here is a revelation, that even now, forty years later, I feel that glorious and horrible weight. But to do justice to that weight I need to share another, more important revelation. And to do that, I have to go back to the very beginning, which is to say I have to fast forward to 1998, after my beloved son Trinity is born, named after these mountains, named after this family story, and how in 1998 at my grandmother's 75th birthday celebration, my father gets this romantic notion to take my brother and I back up to these mountains to harvest a bottle of water from Grizzly Falls for Trinity's baptism.

That summer he goes to the falls with my brother and me, harvests that water, and without us seeing, picks up a stone from the falls and puts it into his pocket. He sews an elk hide pouch around it and burns words into the leather, instructing baby Trinity to take me back into these mountains when he is old enough to carry his own pack. And in 2011, Trinity does. We are all under his grandfather's spell, as likely you are now. Who does such romantic gestures for his family? My father does.

But when my son, my beloved Trinity looks through his binoculars on the morning we are to recreate the correct route up the waterfall to the lake, marked with hard-to-find little stone cairns by previous adventurers up the boulder washout, the look of boyish, wilting concern as he looks from the binoculars to me and then his words, *we're going up, there?* makes my heart fall down the boulder chute and crash at the bottom and just like that, my father's spell is broken.

No, son. Hell no... This is as far as we go. The water here is just as good as it was up there.

And that might be the end of the story, but while time is on our side, let's
go back to where the man and Jasper are sleeping, and the boy which is
me hears a large clumsy movement some 50 feet away. *Hey*, he whispers.
From the sound of movement comes a low series of deep percussive snorts.
Hey! He punches the man's shoulder, waking him. *What?* the man, irritated.
There's a bear in our campsite! The man lifts his head and listens intently.
Nothing. *Bullshit. Bears don't travel this far past the lower meadows.* But
something rumbles inside of the boy's spirit, something nearly masculine
and terrible. *Then why the fuck do they call it Grizzly Lake?*

Good point and the man begins to noisily unzip his sleeping bag. Jasper
rustles invisibly in the dark, *yep that's sumbitch is likely after my supper
again. I'll take care of it.* Among the three of them, none has a flashlight,
but they hear the prospector get out of his sleeping bag and stand upright.
Neither man nor boy is prepared for the three blaring gunshots that follow,
the quick light flashing from the barrel, and the sound that
drowns the entire mountain valley in a rush then
retreats, leaving behind only the sound of the falls and
the boy's heartbeat ringing in his ears like sparrows' wings.

*That ought to take care of any
problems we might have this evening,*
Jasper says as he slowly folds
himself back into his sleeping bag
with what sounds like a sigh of
satisfaction.

57

*

By morning, Jasper, the man, and the boy gather their gear, piss on the remaining coals, then hike out of camp. The man is limping but determined to keep a fast pace. Jasper is rehashing his stories to the man and cackling at his own jokes. The boy, yards behind and slowing already, retreats into himself. He pays little attention to the burden on his back, even less to the hobbled scratching of the man and prospector's footsteps. The boy's feet feel heavier, everything feels heavier. He had been saved, hadn't he? He was sure of his own death, but here he is, snatched away from it, and the boy thinks that the world will never be the same for him, never as simple as running from third base to home plate awash in red polyester jerseys and joyous prepubescent cheers.

I remember my last baseball game of that season in '83. It is the only game my father, who is still my father back then, has ever seen me play. Arriving late in the fifth inning, armed with his camera, he frames me into the batter's box as I swing at everything in three whiffing strikes, *click* wildly trying *click* to hit one over the fence *click* for my dad.

Hutch taps the bill of my hat with affection and tells me to hang in there, that it will be there next time and to be patient and wait for the right pitch. Everything will be okay if I just keep my game simple, and that my swing will not abandon me forever and *yes of course* I am fun to watch. I am worth watching every game. He says that to me. Trademark Clutch Hutch.

The man and Jasper continue down the trail far ahead of the boy. The boy kneels down at the mossy creek side. Leaning under the weight of his pack, he cups his hands into the moving water. The water is so cool and so sweet and so clear that the boy bursts out crying before he can stuff the feeling away. It is a tears and snot, lonesome kind of cry, so hard that he feels his eyelids are turning inside out. Behold the boy. Behold, Jimmy Dicks.

Some people say that time gets away from us, but that just isn't true for me anymore. I mean just look at him, the boy; he's right there by the light of the moving water. Right there just as sure as I am. And so is Trinity, and my brother and my chosen fathers and mothers and the sparrows and now even all of you. That man and Jasper disappeared down the trail without any regard for the boy. So what? The boy is surrounded by a great cloud of witnesses, all of us, windmilling our arms as together we cheer,

C'mon, Jimmy Dicks keep on truckin'. Come on, Jimmy Dicks. Come home—

I'll Give You Something
To Cry About

As the Florida wind bent the trees
and turned the night sky orange,
my father's footsteps pounded
down the thin hallway of our
lemon-yellow trailer toward my
bedroom door, each step the
approaching weather of his voice.

My ear was perched against
the smooth, wood-paneled walls,
the grooves sharp against my
chubby, wet face. Yes, I had been
crying. My mother was crying in
the room next door.

I could hear her fists hammering
the pea-green carpet, the trailer
booming and wailing like incoming
fire. My door punched open
and my father said what he always
said in his very own John Wayne
way, daring me even now to be
a man.

The Death of Old Gods

Ankle deep in the lake from which my sons
were baptized, I rip out bible-thin pages
from your flight manual. I name your divine
rattle and howl for what it is, the guttural
gears churning with the whir of opposing forces.

You, pilot. You hovering beast-angel, you rider
of metal dragons, Godman who has seen all sides
of yonder clouds, you of all should have known better—

The turbulence from your machinations force me
down into this water, the wake pressed down
like fist-punched glass. I call you out, you smooth-stick
villain, my overpowered voice a vapor and then gone.

To hover is not divine, you sanctimonious fop.
Just another of your cyclic and collective tricks.
Even so, despite myself, when some lofty chariot
thunders overhead, my heartbeat rises high
above all other fools who've ever been in love.

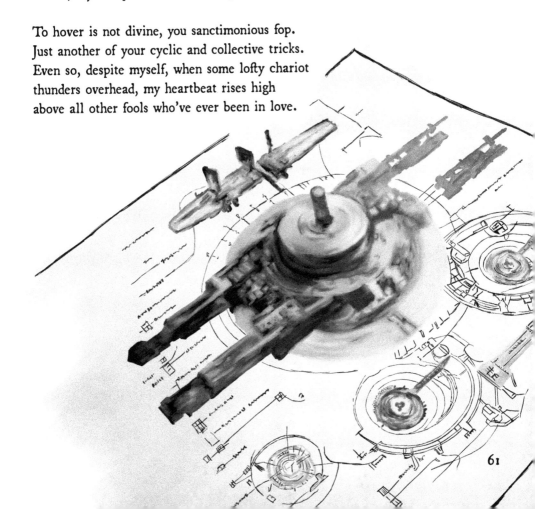

Damnation By Firelight

After roasting marshmallows, the sticky sweet on my children's fingers, my father stares into the coals, starts about his mother, my grandmother, my children's great-grandmother. He tells of how she fought her death to the end, even under the morphine drip. Nonverbal tantrums on her bed.

She must have been staring at the approaching gates of Hell,

he says, in front of my children. His new wife nods solemnly in agreement, though she is too new to have ever met her, my grandmother. She offers some platitude in support of my father, but I cannot hear it at all, no matter how still I try to stay, no matter how still my children try to stay. The blood is firing in my ears, pounding like the hooves of an apocalypse that doesn't come, the words that I would say to shed light on the tantrums on my grandmother's bed, responding to the whispers above her head,

You don't have to call him. Don't tell Jimmy she is dying.

Rage Fu Hustle

Behold, this is the bullshit showdown my father has been avoiding.

Cue the music.
Smash-cut credits.

Jimmy Dicks
   Versus
     THE FATHER

The scene opens and I am already pinned down behind my father's silver bullet trailer, while he, having the high ground, flings scriptures down like arrows. Barrage— the sound each scripture makes against the trailer when it lands, like the beating of an empty trash can. The subtitles read:

[ARROWS PIERCE ARMOR, SEVERE GRUNTING]

Enough. I show myself and bellow "Behold!" like some Old Testament prophet, like that one warrior woman in curlers inhaling her entire cigarette in one breath and *Behoooooooooold, you think you have the high ground!?* My father's big cartoon eyes, another barrage of his arrows but this time they pass right through me, and trumpets sound above his head, an opening in the clouds, gold and light, like Samson in Sunday School, like a flannel board bitch-slap Jesus. The trumpets. The trumpets!

Rush forward. All is quiet. We are both on equal ground. I am wearing the bathrobe I wore in church, the skit about Joseph, dreamer of dreams. We face off, my father and me, a Spaghetti Western Rage Fu Hustle, we are samurai pilgrims at the edge of war. We hold still, apart from the breeze blowing my bathrobe as well as terry cloth can blow, apart from my father's serene white comb-over wind-socking with the falling leaves.

We are still. We are stones.

In slow motion, I begin, from the deep core from below my navel, a bellow— The wind shifts, follows the force of the bellowed leaves, hair, robes blown in the direction of my voice...

My father's ears pin back like a dog about to be beaten, a dog's sad wince in a stiff wind. Have mercy. Lord have mercy upon my father.

The scene goes on but the harder I try to remember what happens the tape ends, bubbles, melts away into light, but a voice, the narrator's voice says, *if you understand the beauty in this, you understand the beauty in your father—*

And I cannot remember anything but *this: a flash of a black and white picture, my father as a child, fat fish in both hands, almost bigger than he is, straining under the weight of his trophy, and to the camera, his young, self-conscious face—*

The Trapper's Son

If you find her
move slowly into her shack.
Shout a greeting from the kitchen

She will lift and empty hand
from an empty boot
once holding a revolver.
She will call you into the living room.

You will smell oregano
as you round the corner.
Witness the woman
in her decomposing chair.

She will tell you
her pelts are gone,
snatched by scavengers,

Lost, she groans, *lost*—
She tracked her boy through the night
through ice and snow,
hypothermic.

She will try to tell you how
she found him huddled there, ivory
statue in the moonlight, how
she touched him, she touched her son
and knew. How the searchers found her
there, lingering upon his frozen lips.

To My Brother Just Over the Mountain

I hope that you will forgive me. I have secreted myself just past your homeward road, only one folded row of mountains between us. I tell myself that two hours driving would be too much to ask of either you or me. It's such short notice. But I know. Two hours is nothing compared to the twelve hours I've already come, and the twelve years that have separated you and me.

Of course, you'd remember our last hike to Avalanche Lake. You lived near Glacier then, and now I hear you've made it as a chef just north of Yellowstone. Of course, you'd remember the mostly rambling gentle up and down in forested hills with intimate creek views until that granite vista of distant braided waterfalls. We didn't work hard to get to the gratuitous view. At the far side of the lake, where the voyeur parade of people grew thin, you may remember how my youngest flung a lure that fizzled into the water and you were teaching Trinity how to tie one of your world famous flies. But then the bushes, the bushes they moved, the bushes right beside me. Beside me the bushes moved and the pulse of the earth shifted by me on padded paws. I was between these bushes and my own cubs and these bushes, these bushes were moving. The golden hump of her fur is what I saw first, just before she broke through.

She halted. We all halted, remember? Including her two yearlings behind her. We all halted, except for our father, who maneuvered slowly away from us. Do you remember that? Later I would remember his tired joke he used to tell us, "I don't have to outrun the bear, I just have to outrun you!"

It wasn't her eyes. The bear's. It was her golden hump of fur that quiet quake-shifted with each step toward us before she halted again. I showed her my hands, outstretched like a sad rodeo clown Jesus. Did I remember that right? Or was it a flash in my head just before I could act? Then back to the bushes and away from the trail, that beautiful sow left with her yearlings.

And the ground did not shake with each footfall, but did you see how I left my body like a sky full of birds, then quickly caterwauled back into my chest as I hen-checked my children close to me and ushered them to lower ground? Did you see how our father peeked over his sunglasses in cavalier nonchalance and said, "Sometimes you eat the bar and sometimes the bar eats you." I know this letter is not about him, but those eyes, our father's, of gleeful detachment...

You may remember that it took two more summers for us to make it official, the permanent silence between him and me. Permanent save for his sporadic cruel epistles scrawled in the Bic pen equivalent of a Founding Father's calligraphy. That beautiful handwriting. What a cruelly squandered gift. There go those wingbeats in my chest again.

Perhaps it is either cruel, or weak, or both to share these feelings in a letter with you, considering that's what started all this trouble in the first place. I'm sorry about that. Ten years. Ten years since those letters. Despite all he has said, I hope you remember that I wasn't trying to turn you against him. The father I had could only love one son at a time. I didn't have to outrun the bear, I just had to outrun you. Leaving was the best I thought I could do. Maybe the father you had was different than that. That would be more relief to me than you could know.

For what it's worth, as the sun set down one last time over your mountains, I stretched my arms out wide, not for any griz this time, but this time out of gratitude for you. For your life now. Yeah. I'm still just as sad as Jesus sometimes. But maybe this time, I hope that what I whispered to the wind with my arms stretched wide will—

Forgive me. I had no idea what I was doing.

The Twenty Dollar Fishing Rod

The Coho "Silver Jack" salmon is known for its furious fight at the end of a hook, a hard-won jewel of the Pacific Ocean. But on this day in 1978, we are land-locked, my grandfather and I, fishing for rainbows at Silver Lake instead. We are just below the fat snow-covered dome of Mt. St. Helens, uninterrupted by the eruptions to come. Two years from now, where we are standing will be under the furious mudflow of ash, earth, logs and debris. The lake is silent, save for the whir of the line flying out with each of my grandfather's casts, the slow reeling in, the responsive tug and ebb from the tip of the rod as he turns the reel. I step back, mesmerized by his motion, forgetting that I have left my rod on the dock. I step back and the spell is broken, the lure jingling the alarm of my trespass. My grandfather jerks his attention to me, looks down at my feet. "Jesus Christ, Jimmy! That's my twenty-dollar fishing rod!" My eight-year-old face screws itself up to cry. My grandfather's voice grows softer, as he rubs the flannel of my back, "Aw, don't do that buddy." He reassures me with a firm pat on my back and kisses my forehead. His whiskered face. A hint of coffee on his breath.

This to me is mercy. Just like when, each summer, bobbing in my grandfather's boat at the yawning mouth of the Columbia River, I would cry "Fish on!" just before hurling my innards over the side. And my grandfather would laugh as he reeled in the fish as we bobbed and churned on the river's surface. He called me his good luck charm, his perfect fishing buddy because I would feed the fish and he would catch them.

Flash forward, my grandfather in a blue hospital gown, blue as the sky overhead. His mouth gaped open like a fish out of water, the labored breathing, the lacerated tongue from when he seized the night before. Mercy is how he almost opened his eyes when I touched his shoulder and whispered, "Hey Grandpa, it's Jimmy Dicks," how his sealed eyelids couldn't

hide his spirited irises as they moved wildly like salmon beneath the water's surface. Mercy is his wondrous groan of recognition at my name, as if witnessing a big fish rising from the deep, and the blush on my lips as I kissed his forehead, which was soft as a newborn's skin. And mercy, good god, is the twenty-dollar fishing rod given to me days after he died. Not the rod of justice, but of mercy, a barbed hook reeling in blessings from the unknown deep.

The Coho "Silver Jack" salmon is known for its furious fight at the end of a hook, but my grandfather didn't fight like that in the end. Peacefully, he surrendered into the deep, and he took so much of me with him.
So I cast and I cast with my twenty-dollar fishing rod, hoping to find again what I have lost.

Lord have mercy.

I'm worthy of the sacred space I take
tending to my every mistake.
Vigilant I stand upon my shadow
waking up and picking up the weight.

I will rise alongside
those who in the darkness carry my light.

*   -Sparrow "Legacy"*

Wine-Dark Mother

I

And I am waiting,
standing in front of a thick
scarlet curtain, a rippling wall.

Light spills down in threes.
I stand alone in the shadows
of the stage, my back to the audience,
and teeter toward a rapid-eye sequence.

I am waiting, darkened,
waiting for something to begin—

Sensation:
Stillness. Cabernet diving *where?*
I don't remember what I am waiting for
waiting? am I? Scarlet ridges fade
into copper plains, to the pale peach
of and Autumn sky just after sunset

just after a long rain.
It has been raining. It must have
been raining here for days. My knees
soaked cold, press into the familiar,
familial? grass, as I kneel again
beside my father's gravesite. Why

do I keep coming here, keep coming
to this place? but something is different now.

What was that noise? That singing through the fog?

Why do I keep coming to this place when I refuse to come back?
Whatever we say *no* to
comes back and sticks
to us a little bit

like a dragon with seven heads,
like a Romanian folktale.

Is there anyone in the audience
who can hear me,
anyone with a compass?

A light?

2

A flute sings over the water,
a swallow skirting on a ribbon
of wind. And here I am, *where?*
walking down some road,
brick pavers, cobblestone walks,
yellow leaves decaying. The river
whispers by, a mallard with his satin
emerald head *emblem?* swims
away from me, forming a V
of his own, a V of ripples
glowing toward the farther shore
to a lone tree, growing crimson.

A pale blue sky.
Deadened wind. Butterflies
dust my face, brushing my cheeks
as the sky stains itself, deep cranberry.

Do not touch them, do not rub
their fragile dust. Your oily hands
would rend their wings, render them flightless.

A cymbal. A gong—
Butterflies disappear.

The shadows
of the greening rain
come shouting down.
A figure— a figure stands
on the opposite shore, her silken robes
spill out from the opening of her woolen cloak
flagging, bannering in the wind.
The ornate copper streetlights start to glow,
she comes, floating toward me in the rain.

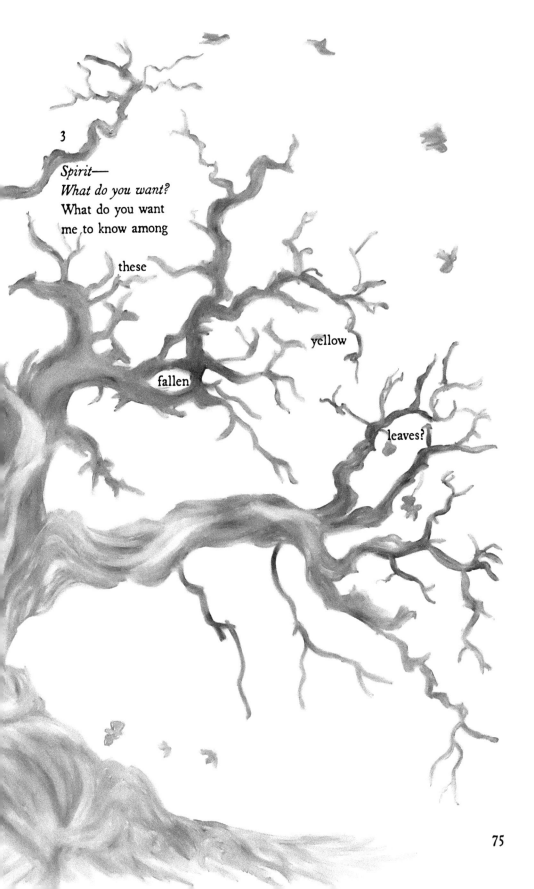

3

Spirit—
What do you want?
What do you want
me to know among

these

yellow

fallen

leaves?

4

The rains have stopped again.
pale lavender light reflects from the water,
the dimpled cups of water,
as if frozen in mid snowmelt.

5

Spirit—
it is getting colder
and the geese are crying
in the water,

preparing to make their way
South. Can you tell me

why,

why this is always the season
always the season I want to fall

in love?

6

A path between us forms,
myself, this figure
on the farther shore.

No Jacob's ladder, no
warlike angel who fights
with me in shafts of staining light.

Just a pull, as if I were
a floating man in space
umbilically drawn toward her.

Soon she is upon me, face veiled
in darkness, smudged and blurred
from my periphery.

Dizzy, I cannot
bring myself to rise
up from my knees, and now

she holds a globe of water
above my head, a globe
which shudders
in her delicate

nightmare hands—

7

Cupped in her nightmare hands,
tapered fingers, the globe,
a giant milky dew drop.

  Her fingertips
  barely touch
  the orb
  and where
  they touch
  a channel
  of tears
  flows down.

Water rains out.
Compromised membrane
where her fingers
touch, but the orb
retains its shape.
Its watermark
does not go down.

The sky releases rain,
releases rain again.

8

Piano strains begin
to tinkle up and down,
down and up in minor
scales. Percussive.

Fleeting. Something
bass within my spine
swells up to meet this
troubled and trebled
rhythm.

Fugue state logic begs me
to *concentrate, this detail is important.*

Pine needles, like the ones
where they abused you
underneath that yellow trailer
needles strewn about the grass
now with the scat of geese
who plan to punish you again
abandoning the shoreline
while the swans above—

unmolested, stay nearby,
remaining light
upon the water.

9

Without a voice,
I hear the woman call
to me:

Look into the globe of water
look and you will find it find
a portal to the outside world

Rise and look and you will find it.
Look into the globe of water—

10

Remember when your father said
your head was lodged so far
up where the sun stopped shining
that you needed this here porthole
in your belly button just to see the world?

Despite all his cleverness,
here's what you could always see
that he had no capacity to see:

I look and see—

Behold, it is my mother, the face of my mother, young and sleeping. I am
three years old, in love and watching her sleep. Her eyes are closed, as if
remembering a tune, as if she could summon better memories or dreams.
Inside her is a stillness that I've never seen before, a stillness exorcising
roiled screams like wounded pigs fresh-bound for slaughter. Now, but now
she is so still, sublime, and now this watery porthole is no longer weeping.
I am three years old watching her face so closely, minutes without move-
ment, breathing, then a shadow realization:

Is she dead?

11

Gone—

The membrane gives way, the orb
soaks my feet, my pant legs, the boy
who wet himself with fear. I look up
and the figure's blurry veil is gone.

It is my mother. The ghost of my mother
the ghost of the mother she wishes she was,
face frozen in bronze. Eyes closed, lips pursed
as if waiting for a kiss—

Where pale, lavender light
reflects from the water,
the dimpled cups of water

as if frozen in the Autumn snow,
I will stay, stay with you here
in this dream dear Mother. Mother,
I will stay here with you sleeping
she is only sleeping!

Mother, this is who
you wanted to be. This
is who you promised you'd be.

This is who you promised you'd be.

Black Madonna
Villae Populi, Romania

They moved in like a path of swans
those Carmelite nuns who weaved
toward the orphans' concrete bridge.

We were a line of hands,
calloused, passing buckets of cement
to pour into concrete forms.

They glided over hard-packed sunlight
and spills of wet cement, to hand
a Mother's medal to her children.

One sister reached toward my face,
both palms cupped upward, ebony fingers,
dark flames offered up in praise.

She cupped my cheeks in silence. Smiled.
I welled up like an abandoned fountain
at the bottom of a well— I heard

a whisper in my head, *Good Teacher.*
My cheeks were burning, my chest a rising sob
as if I, as if mine were the face of God.

Her Wounded Side

What I love most
is this scar, running
a rough diagonal down
your abdomen,
torn open the day
your father died.

Such a wound
would freeze another shut
but you, your belly soft and warm.

Naked on my knees
I touch your wounded side.

My Lord.
My God.

I love to trace this scar
with the tip of my nose,
slide my lips
down that fleshy rope
marbled and thick,
umbilical cords
that nourish our children.

This scar, from where
they reached into your organs
after shocking you back to life,
but now, your belly soft and warm—

Revocation

Forgiveness is the release of all hope for a better past—
forgiveness is for everybody needing safe passage through my mind.

-Buddy Wakefield

And herein lies the revocation,
the cancellation of the debt,
the jubilee annulment.

Herein lies my surrender,
my retirement, my withdrawal
of all the charges.

Let them drop into the wishing well
with no more hope for wishes
other than to wish my father well.

Farewell Poem to a Living Father

Goodbye, dear man.
Fold these words
into your pocket
in case you need

      safe passage.

We wish you

      rest
         relief

with this paper boat,
this lit candle for you

beneath this full
paper moon.

We let you go
from these shores
to the outgoing tide.

And if you and I
were both wrong
about forgiveness,
in how it comes, or
how it goes—

take this folded paper
and give it to the boatman
when he asks you

      if you were loved.

ACKNOWLEDGEMENTS

Eight years ago, there were still some broken pieces in the First Edition left to sift through, reimagine and make anew into something stronger than what they were before the breaking. Some poems after the writing felt almost like curses hanging over my head; not the intended purpose, so I tore them from the book, set them alight, and let them float away.

Other broken pieces not originally in the book fused together to bend the arc more toward a hard-won healing. I have my loved ones to thank for that, especially my grown children. I am more my true self when I am with them.

I am so grateful to Paul Grimsley, my publisher at *Musehick Publications,* who believed that this book was not only worthy of being published once, but twice. This Illustrated Second Edition feels like the more fully realized version of itself, and the challenge of illustrating it was a great meditation for me to see the work anew and live through it again. I hope these new pages add to your reading experience. Today, this book feels more like a talisman of healing for me rather than a memorial to what has been lost. I used to feel like I was inflicting this book on my readers rather than blessing them with it. Now, I can't wait to place it into your hands.

A few of these works appeared in other publications. I am grateful to *Fire Magazine* for publishing "Jacob Wrestling", *Vain* for publishing "Ashes", *The Good Men Project* for publishing "Rage Fu Hustle" and "Damnation By Firelight" and *Press 1 Quarterly* for publishing both "Snoopyland" and an earlier version of "Son of Abraham."

Finally, anyone who is blurbed by necessary luminaries like Jessamyn Smyth, Ilya Kaminsky and Katie Farris undoubtedly knows what it is like to be humbled by such rare and generous praise. And when Katie referred to my work as "the unmaking of a chosen son, the birth of a good man," she gave me an aspiration that will take the rest of my life to hopefully achieve.

And to you, the reader: thank you for seeing me. I hope this book helps you to see yourself better after having read it. You are necessary and beautiful and more rare than you ought to be.

Thank you for reading.

Much love,

Jim Churchill-Dicks

Printed in the USA
CPSIA information can be obtained
at www.ICGtesting.com
LVHW021925240724
786348LV00004B/61

9 781953 527615